CRICKET GUIDE

by
Bob Farmer

with additional records by
Ron Wills

HAMLYN
London · New York · Sydney
Toronto

Contents

Cricket – an appreciation

If mad dogs and Englishmen went out in the mid-day sun, it might have served Mr Noel Coward to add a verse or two on the sanity of those who invented the game of cricket in this country.

There could hardly have been a more inappropriate birthplace for a sport which relies so heavily on good weather.

But irrationality is one of the charms of cricket. It is ever unpredictable and few sports if any produce such sudden changes of fortune in the course of a match.

It has the subtlety of chess, the excitement of a race and the grace of old age. It is a team game played by individual talents.

It is a relic of the British Empire and, for a relic, the old game is looking remarkably healthy.

But it was not always that way. Indeed, after the last war, as television and motor cars started crowding into people's lives, cricket suffered the cold shoulder from the many thousands who had previously flocked to matches.

By the early 1960s, cricket had reached a crisis. Championship matches were being played to a bare handful of hardy followers, even the Test matches had lost appeal.

Something had to be done if many counties were not to drift into bankruptcy and indeed something was done. Sponsored limited overs cricket was introduced in the form of the Gillette Cup knockout competition in 1963. It was 'instant' cricket and it was an instant success. Crowds who had tired of the inconclusive three-day game could now see a match settled in a day and often in the most thrilling manner.

There was no looking back. In 1969 the John Player Sunday League came into being, in 1972 another knockout competition – the Benson and Hedges Cup.

The crowds flocked back in their thousands, counties kept reporting attendance records, the Tests benefited from the general resurgence of interest and television, instead of being an enemy, became a missionary for cricket.

It is all a far cry from 1272 when Edward the First's son was mentioned as playing Creag, from 1598 when a manuscript mentioned the Surrey coroner 'playing at crickett' from Hambledon Cricket Club, the White Conduit Club, Thomas Lord and Doctor Grace. But they would all have been happy to think that in 1975 cricket has a popularity that has not been surpassed.

Batting

Equipment

A bad workman will always blame the tools of his trade for a poor performance. For a bad batsman these same limp excuses cannot be made provided a few simple principles are observed in the choice and care of his equipment.

The basics for a batsman are, of course, a bat, a pair of pads and gloves and a box.

In selecting your bat, the size and weight are of the utmost importance. Never use a bat that feels too heavy; always find the weight and length that matches your strength and height.

Ideally a man of 5 ft 9 in or more will use a bat 2 ft 11 in long and 2·4 lb heavy — and a school-boy between 5 ft 3 in and 5 ft 5 in will bat with one 2 ft 9 in to 2 ft 10 in and weighing 2·2 to 2·3 lb.

Having selected the bat, it is also important to treat it with care. Use linseed oil on the face about half-way down where the ball is most often going to strike. The bat should always be oiled when dry, but don't overdo it. When the surface becomes so hard that it does not soak in the oil, use a scraper to remove the film off the surface.

Batting pads are merely a question of comfort, while gloves are important. At a lower level of the game, fast bowlers may be no demons. The better the standard, the faster the bowling and the more important your gloves.

Stance and grip

The correct way to grip your bat is to have both hands close together and reasonably high on the handle. The reason is that if the bat is held lower down the handle, your leverage is reduced and the reach and swing reduced, too.

The left hand is above the right (for a left-handed batsman the position is reversed) with the back of the left hand facing towards the bowler with both thumbs around the handle. Use all the fingers of the left hand to grip the bat because this hand has to control the movement of the bat.

After the grip the stance, and here comfort is the key. Either foot should be able to move freely, so the weight should be distributed evenly between both feet. It does not really matter whether the feet are put together or a little apart.

The shoulders should be pointed down the pitch towards the bowler, otherwise a two-eyed stance will occur wherein the left shoulder, instead of pointing at the bowler, points towards mid-on making the stance open. It is certainly not an uncommon stance in cricket, but it has the disadvantage of making the shot to the off-side that much more difficult to execute with real freedom.

Eyes and wrists
The eyes are used first to establish the type of ball that is coming as soon as possible after it leaves the hand of the bowler. To see the ball correctly, the two eyes must be at the same distance from the ball — that is to say with the head facing directly down the wicket.

The idea is to be able to judge where the ball is likely to pitch, giving early indication of the type of delivery and maximum time to decide on the stroke to be played.

Timing depends on the flexibility of the wrists. They should never be kept stiff for this would limit the strength of a stroke.

Use of the wrists in making a stroke is as follows: the bat is lifted back at first by bending the wrists and arms and as the ball is played on the downward movement, the arms move first and the wrists come into action just before the ball is hit.

The wrists can also correct errors of timing in the arm movement. If the arms have brought the bat down too soon, then a slow movement of the wrists will delay the bat in the last stage before theb all arrives.

Likewise. if the arms bring the bat down too late, very speedy movement of the wrists can get the bat there in time. In fact use of the wrists in the vital instant before impact decides the ability of a batsman.

Concentration

Concentration might seem an elementary aspect of batting. but many wickets fall because a batsman relaxes on seeing a bad ball, lifts his head and does not follow the flight.

Remember always to watch the ball. From the moment that the bowler starts to run in the batsman must watch the ball. Even if he finds it hard to make scoring strokes, he will be very hard to dismiss if his concentration is sound.

With concentration comes commitment which means making the decision on how to play the ball. As it approaches the ball can do many strange things, either through the air or off the

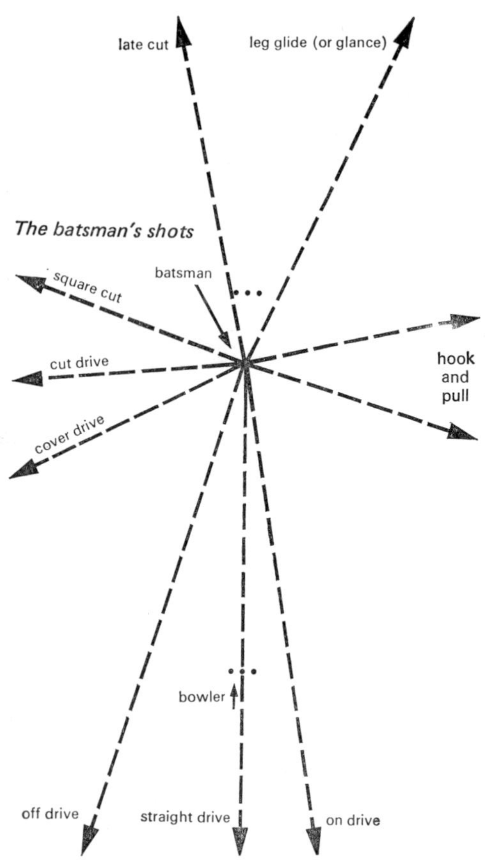

late cut
leg glide (or glance)
The batsman's shots
square cut
batsman
cut drive
hook
and
pull
cover drive
bowler
off drive
straight drive
on drive

Forward defensive
stroke: head well
forward, with left hand

*doing the leading,
left knee bent and
eyes well over the ball.*

ground. Thus it is wise for the batsman not to commit himself until he has learnt all he can about the ball.

The time to make a stroke depends on the speed of footwork. Many batsmen commit themselves far too early and can be trapped by a late deviation of the delivery.

A disciplined batsman will always wait as long as he can before committing himself to the stroke.

It is a useful hint to have someone serve the ball from half-way down the wicket in practice. It gives the batsman no time to move too early and can only improve his technique.

Forward stroke

The forward stroke is designed to deal with a delivery that can be reached before or just after it has pitched.

All the weight is put on the right foot, leaving

the left foot free to move forward. The left hand controls the bat's movement which should be held with a short backlift.

Then, just as the bat starts coming down, the left foot should be advanced close to the pitch of the ball with the body's weight transferred.

At the point of contact the left leg is bent at the knee while the right foot just touches the ground with the toe just inside the batting crease to avoid the possibility of a sharp stumping chance should the ball be missed.

The left shoulder nearly touches the left ear, head is well forward with eyes level directly in line with the bat handle and the ball is met directly beneath the eyes.

Most common fault in the forward stroke is not to get far enough down the wicket to the pitch of the ball and failing to get the left foot on the line of flight of the ball. If the ball is played in front of the left leg instead of alongside it, the result is that a simple catch is often popped up for the bowler as he follows through after delivering the ball.

Back stroke
Although the forward stroke is not only a model method of defence but also capable of producing handsome scoring shots, the back stroke is just as important to the well-equipped batsman.

This stroke is for deliveries that cannot be reached on the front foot — or, indeed, for an exceptionally overpitched full toss.

If the ball pitches at an awkward length then the batsman can do little more than play back in

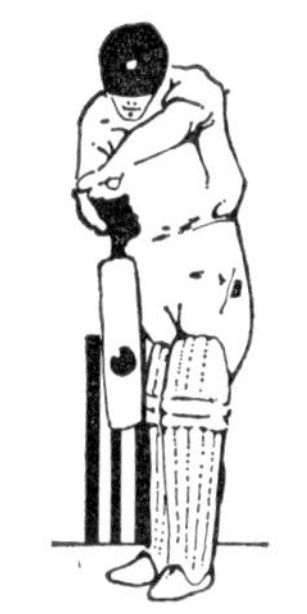

Back defensive stroke

defence of his wicket. If it pitches short, however, then there is plenty of time to lean back, watch the ball onto the bat and punch it away for an often very effective scoring shot.

Footwork and body balance are just as important as with the forward stroke, except that the footwork process is reversed. Thus, the weight must be transferred to the left foot as the right leg is moved back with bat uplifted. The head as ever should be on line with the ball with eyes level and left shoulder and elbow high, the left hand controlling the bat with the right hand grip relaxed.

The ball is met immediately below the eyes with the weight of the body on the back foot. The right foot should be well back towards the stumps, but parallel to the crease.

The Drive
There is no better sight than the perfectly executed drive — for striker and spectator alike.

The off drive.

The shot consists of an almost complete swing of the bat to hit the ball immediately after it has pitched.

There are two basic methods of playing the stroke. If the ball is well up to the batsman, then the left foot advances while the right foot remains rooted in the crease. If the ball is pitched shorter, the batsman can advance down the wicket to meet the ball on the half-volley.

Commitment, discussed earlier, plays an important part in executing the drive. No thoughts of being stumped must enter the batsman's head, otherwise any hesitation will probably mean a failure to get to the pitch of the ball.

With the first method of driving – that is with the right foot remaining grounded – there are some differences to the ordinary forward stroke.

The bat is raised with a much higher uplift, both hands should grip the handle tightly and a turn of the wrists makes the blade face point when the bat is at the top of the lift.

The on drive.

The step with the left foot is not so long, the body is fairly upright and the left leg is unbent. The bat must travel in the direction that the ball will take and stay on this course after the ball has actually been hit. The weight of the body should continue to travel in the direction of the shot with the left shoulder and hip remaining firm (and not swinging round as in a golf swing) with the right shoulder released so that when the full stroke has been completed the batsman's chest should be facing the bowler.

Moving out to drive means taking a long stride down the pitch with the left foot, with the right foot gliding up behind the left heel so that the feet are crossed. The weight is then transferred to the right foot from where the normal drive is played. If, after all this, the batsman realises he is unable to make the ball into a half-volley, the intended drive must be altered into an orthodox forward stroke, otherwise the ball will be spooned into the air.

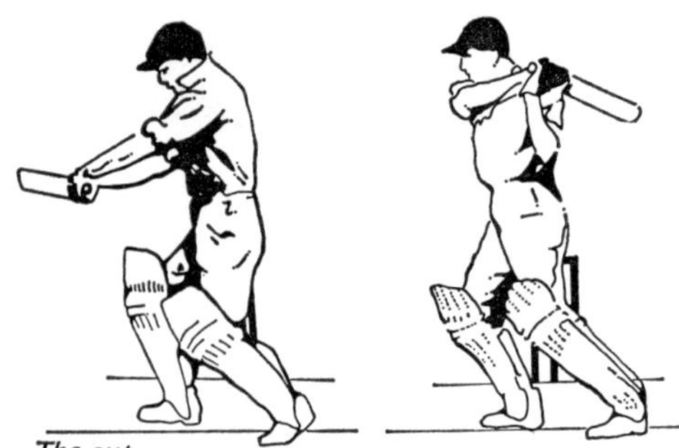
The cut.

The cut

The cut comes into the category known as cross-batted strokes and played with the right foot moving across the wicket and the ball normally being played behind the fielder at point.

Square cuts will probably travel down to third man and late cuts along the ground past second slip.

It is not an easy shot to play and should not really be attempted before the batsman has been in some time and is seeing the ball well.

Most effective deliveries for the cut are medium pace short balls well to the off and the technique is to lift the bat well up – as in the case of the drive – moving the right foot back towards the wicket and facing the off-side just behind point.

Wait for the ball almost to be past the bat and then bring the arms abruptly down, hoping to hit the ball well up on the bat. The weight travels firmly on to the right foot and the bat is thrown hard at the ball in the direction the ball will take.

The arms should be straightened and the wrists quite unflexed.

One point to remember – it is extremely unwise to try the cut against a slow bowler for not many runs will accrue and quite often a catch may be given to a lurking slip.

Hook and pull

In the case of both the hook and the pull, the shot is again a cross-batted one except that, unlike the cut, it is designed to hit short deliveries to leg.

The hook is employed with a short-pitched ball coming at some speed and at a fair height.

This means that there is not much time to play the shot – a most spectacular stroke which will invariably produce a boundary – and speedy footwork is of the essence.

The right foot should be moved back and to the off so that it is outside the line of flight of the ball whereas the head and shoulders are in line and facing the bowler.

The bat is lifted out towards third man and then swept across the body and if correctly timed will prove a powerful shot.

It is, however, a shot for the adventurous batsman and should not be attempted before the pace of the wicket and bowler have been thoroughly decided.

It is also something of a 'sucker' ball from fast bowlers who deliberately bowl short at batsmen with an aptitude for hooking.

Frequently, at the highest level of cricket, Test Match bowlers 'buy' wickets by tempting aggressive batsmen into hooking and skying a catch to the deep fielder.

The pull stroke, on the other hand, is a considerably safer shot to play although not so spectacular as the hook.

It is used either to attack the slow bowler — particularly in pulling with a leg break — or to take advantage of a wicket with no life in it.

Again the right foot should move back and outside the line of flight of the ball which brings the head and shoulders into line with the ball.

The bat is taken up high and comes down at the ball with the batsman's body facing a bit more to the off-side than in the hook shot.

The stroke is played well in front of the body and as the bat moves from off to leg, the weight is transferred to the left foot which will be in advance of the right.

Result is a fairly hard-hit shot somewhere in the region between square leg and midwicket.

Scoring to leg

The legside should be where a vast majority of runs are scored in cricket and unless he bowls the leg break, no bowler willingly aims at the legside. Yet many runs are lost by batsmen who have not learned the art of legside play.

The ball to leg so often seems the signal for a batsman to lose concentration, stop looking at the ball and swing or wave wildly.

For most legside balls, the action to take is a modification of the forward or back strokes.

If the ball is well pitched up a forward stroke is played with the left leg kept out of the way. This is to enable the bat to swing across and hit the ball in front of square leg, with the right foot pivoting round. For shorter balls on or just outside the leg stump play the backstroke and for really wide balls use a crossbat method.

From the leg push a lot of singles and twos should accrue. The shot is made from the shorter ball with the batsman moving his feet for the backstroke with the right foot facing down the wicket and the left shoulder turned towards mid-wicket. That way the ball can be pushed or guided into a gap between legside fielders. For the faster short ball the shot becomes a flick or glide fine down the leg side.

The crossbat shot to leg is otherwise known as the sweep.

Arm movement is a natural swing across the body with the right hand doing all the controlling of the bat. The left leg should be well across, both elbows should be bent so that the ball can be hit with the full face of the bat and aimed in front of square leg. And keep the bat swinging slightly downwards or the ball will swing into the hands of a grateful fielder.

The sweep can be made to look somewhat ungainly if badly executed and this gives cause to confusion with the good old-fashioned cowshot so beloved of village green cricketers.

The difference between the correct sweep and cowshot, in fact, is that the first is played to a ball already pitching outside the leg stump, whereas the cowshot comes from trying to swing the ball round to leg from a delivery on line with middle or off stump. an almighty heave, much favoured by tail-end batsmen with few pretensions to correct strokeplay.

The cowshot can come off, but only employ it if the situation of the match demands a hectic scramble for runs.

Balls to watch
An attacking batsman who keeps the score ticking over is always attractive to watch, but without a sound defensive technique his stay at the wicket will be far more brief than that of the careful batsman. And this means being able to pick out the balls of which to be wary.

A bowler will normally aim for a good length ball which means that after bouncing it can only be struck by the upper half of the bat from which part the drive cannot be executed and which makes scoring difficult when on line with the stumps or passing outside.

If the ball is passing the off stump then the batsman is wise to raise his bat and allow it through to the wicket-keeper without playing a stroke. Any attempt to do so will probably result in the ball finding the outside edge of the bat and snicking a catch to keeper or the slip fielders.

If the ball is on line, the bat should be kept in a vertical position – playing a straight bat.

Another good length ball which signals danger for the batsman is the one pitched up to land just about on the crease. This is the yorker intended to squeeze under the bottom of the bat and take the stumps. The batsman must drop his wrists fast to play it on the base of the bat and 'dig it out'.

Facing the quickie

For somewhat painfully obvious reasons, the inexperienced batsman far prefers facing slow bowling to the paceman. He has the fear of being hit on an unprotected part of the body or even the head if the ball is flying around in spiteful conditions.

But, although he may not be aware of it, there is another reason for his reluctance to face fast bowling – the fact that really quick bowlers are relatively rare and thus he has limited opportunity to learn to play the 'quickie'.

Most fast bowlers will miss the stumps unless they bowl yorkers or very short-pitched balls and the logic is to play forward with a firm grip if the ball is on line, thus making it extremely difficult for the bowler to hit the stumps.

But, at the same time, fast bowlers tend to concentrate on balls that are not intended to hit the wickets in the hope that by trying a stroke the batsman will edge a catch behind to wicket-keeper or slips. It is wise to leave well alone and only play the balls that have to be played, especially in the early stage of an innings, when the batsman is still judging the pace of the wicket.

Playing and missing, however, is inevitable at times when the bowler delivers a ball that might or might not clip the off-stump.

If all this sounds as though the fast bowler is always in the ascendancy, then it is not the case. The batsman has the advantage of not needing to hit hard or swing lustily to be assured of runs since the ball already has pace.

To score off the fast bowler, take these tips:

every short ball at least a foot outside the off-stump can be cut for four; every ball pitched down the legside can be glided to fine leg for one or four; and every half-volley can be driven back straight and will probably beat the field for sheer speed.

And remember that although the wicket-keeper will be waiting for a snick, he has to stand so far back to the genuine fast bowler that the batsman can move forward confident that there is no chance of being stumped.

So, although he must always be wary in the early stages of an innings, the batsman can start counter-attacking the 'quickie' once he has settled in and judged the pace of the wicket.

Facing the slow bowler
The state of the wicket is the all-important factor in the playing of slow bowling.

If the sun shines and the wicket is hard, then few problems should be encountered since the ball will not turn much more than an inch or so in a yard. It does, however, come off the pitch much faster and therefore the good length delivery should always be played on the forward stroke making it into a half-volley. Never go back to this ball — lbw or bowled would be a likely result.

On a soft, slow wicket the spinner becomes more dangerous, although the ball will come off the pitch only slowly. Thus, play back to most balls and the ball can be watched right on to the bat.

The slow bowler really comes into his own on

a sticky pitch or a worn patch of the wicket. The ball turns very sharply and the batsman must be on constant guard. It is now even more helpful to know which way the ball is going to turn and this is done by watching the bowler's hand as he delivers.

If the ball comes from the front of the hand it will be a leg-break from a left-arm bowler and an off-break from a right-armer. From the back of the bowler's hand, the turn will be reversed. Move out to smother the break where possible. When forced to play back get your pads behind your bat.

Above all, in the playing of slow bowling, the use of the feet is vital either in moving out to smother or in turning a ball into a full pitch. The feet are moved in the method for playing a forward drive as earlier described.

Every time you go out and make a ball into a full pitch you should be able to drive effectively.

And if the slow bowler pitches a ball short the batsman can drive, square cut or pull to great effect.

The slow bowler's essential is to drop on to a good length. The batsman can counteract that by the use of his feet.

Calling and running

There is nothing more frustrating for a batsman than to be run out by a fielder, although with the incidence of limited-overs cricket the casualty rate is remarkably high. This, however, is understandable since a mad chase for runs inevitably leads to 'suicidal' singles being risked.

But in the ordinary course of cricket events a run out should be a rarity and to make it uncommon the batsman must learn the correct art of calling and running.

The object of calling is for the batsman in the best position to judge to inform his partner as soon as possible whether a run is or is not possible.

'Yes', 'Come On' or 'One' are the common calls where runs are available; 'Wait' means that the caller wants to make certain before committing himself to a run; 'No' is self-explanatory. In all events the call should be made loud and clear.

The question of who should call depends on the path of the ball. If the striking batsman plays a shot in front of the wicket then logically he has the full field of vision and should make the decision; if the ball is played behind the wicket then the batsman at the non-striker's end takes responsibility for the decision.

The decision on running is determined by several factors. A slow-moving ball wide of a fielder can produce a run, a harder-hit shot may not; the angle at which the ball approaches the fielder; the speed with which the striking batsman can get off the mark — he may, after all, have overbalanced in making his stroke; any knowledge acquired of a particular fielder's prowess.

In being ready to run, the non-striker should leave his crease as the ball is bowled and be on his toes poised to run or return to his ground.

In the actual running, a shot that is an obvious safe single means that the batsman does not need to hare down the wicket, but where there may be a chance of a second run, then the first should be run at top-speed.

Finally, a batsman should not forget that his bat adds to the distance he can travel in the quickest time possible. He does not need to take his feet anywhere near the crease, provided the bat is extended to the full length of the arm and slid over the crease.

Sliding of the bat over the line saves any number of run-outs where a sharp run is taken yet it is surprising how many batsmen — well-known ones at that — tear down the wicket gripping their bat half-way down the handle and held at hip-height.

Bowling

When all is said and done about cricket the art of the game really amounts to the battle of wits between batsman and bowler.

It is the bowler's job to dismiss the batsman either by having him bowled, leg before wicket, caught, stumped or, in rare cases, causing him to play back so abruptly that he hits his own wicket with his bat or some part of his body.

The batsman, on the other hand, has two functions — first, to avoid being dismissed, second, to amass runs.

It is the bowler, in fact, who holds the initiative since he determines the type of delivery — fast, medium-pace or slow. That said, the bowler also determines whether the ball be difficult or easy to play.

The difficult ball is one that should make the batsman think that, if he misses it, it will hit his wicket. This is known as good direction. But the ball should be pitched so that it arrives at an awkward angle to the bat, thereby possibly causing an unintended shot. This is referred to as good length.

The easy ball is regarded as one of three types. Firstly comes the full toss — a ball projected up so high that the batsman can hit it before it pitches. Then comes the half-volley which can be hit immediately after pitching. And finally the long hop — a ball pitched very short, say half-way down the wicket — which gives the batsman ample time to see it on to his bat and punch it away to just about any point he chooses.

On the following few pages we will look at the art of length and direction and of the various methods of bowling. It is worth considering, before going into the technique of good bowling, that although the batsman may seem to have the more glamorous part to play, to the expert eye there is no better sight in cricket than a master bowler demonstrating his art, be he fast, medium or slow.

The run-up
The purpose of a good run-up is to bring the bowler smoothly to the wicket with the correct speed for his style of delivery.

It takes much practice to decide on the length of a run-up and the bowler must go through the motion time and again until it has become automatic.

Even the greatest bowlers can look less than smooth at the start of a run-up. Some develop an untidy shuffling mannerism to start with. It does not matter, provided that after the start of the run-up, the paces are smooth and even.

Any shuffle half-way to the wicket means that the previous part of the run is a waste of time and energy. For example, for fast and medium-pace bowlers, the run must work up its pace and not be checked just before the delivery. Any inclination to do that and the bowler might just as well not have bothered running at all.

The delivery
When the bowler has reached on his run-up the point of delivery, the following action should occur (we are still talking in terms of the right-handed bowler – reverse the procedure for the left-armer).

The basic bowling action.

The right leg has arrived at the ground just behind the crease with the foot facing almost square to the leg side, with the left shoulder facing the batsman.

The left leg advances on the vital step. As it leaves the ground it is facing mid on, but as the body swing starts it pivots before landing to point towards square leg.

The body swing is generated by the run-up and work of the left arm which is raised almost vertically with the bowler looking down the wicket over the top of the left arm.

As the left foot comes to the ground, the left arm is cut away to develop the swing of the body.

The left foot comes down hard, with the left left leg straight as the right shoulder swings forward in delivery. Meanwhile, the right foot has left the ground and is coming through on its next step, the first of the follow-through.

Obviously, the ball should be delivered from as great a height as possible which means that the vertical distance between left foot and right-hand fingers should be as much as possible at the point of delivery.

Length and direction
Good-length bowling is the essential for a successful bowler. A rough estimate of just what constitutes a good length delivery is to pitch between six and seven yards from the batsman's wicket if bowling fast; five yards if medium pace; and four yards if slow. These distances represent the 'no man's land' between the forward and back strokes.

Control of length depends on an easy rhythmic delivery and persistent practice. The ball, as previously mentioned, should be released from the highest point that the hand can reach. Thus the delivery will be smooth, not jerky, and control of length will be the greater.

Together with length comes variation in direction. The ball that is always on line with the stumps starts to become easy to play. The batsman has only to play straight down the line.

But the batsman can be kept guessing if some balls come straight, some just outside the off stump and others on or just wide of the leg stump.

The best way to learn length and then direction is perhaps to place a piece of newspaper on the target area and see how many times it can be hit in a six-ball over. Keep plugging away to improve the score.

Variety of pace

Assuming that the art of the run-up, the delivery, the length and direction have now been mastered, the bowler who is going to become a most proficient wicket-taker will have to develop an ability to vary the pace of his delivery, be he fast or slow.

It is, perhaps, the hardest part of his education since he must achieve pace variation without tipping off the batsman by changing his run-up and style of delivery in any apparent way.

It is also a most effective way of trapping the batsman who, having accustomed himself to the bowler's arc of flight, may now play too early or too late with fatal results.

The trick is in the extent to which the wrist is used in the final phase of the delivery.

What is required is a very slight change of pace with no change of action. If the bowler flicks his wrist to full capacity then the ball will come through that bit faster; if he does not use his wrist at all then the ball will be that much slower.

Watching a bowler changing pace from a side-view vantage point, the trick is fairly easy to see. But for the batsman facing the bowler, it stays a disguise if correctly operated.

Spin

Fast bowlers may be the front line of a fielding team's attack, having first use of the new ball and gathering their wickets in spectacular style.

But the spin bowler is the stylist. Where the fast bowler relies on sheer speed and swerve, the spinner is the subtle tactician involved in a battle of wits with the batsman.

He may sometimes be hit when there is nothing in the wicket for him. but he should always be encouraged for he is the backbone of the attack.

Spin bowling is basically about producing a change of direction after the ball has pitched. It may change direction from the legside (a leg break), from the off (off break) or speed straight off the pitch (top spin).

But before embarking on the methods of bowling the off and leg break, it is as well to know the best conditions in which they can be employed.

The spinner does not need the ball still to have its early shine although it should be dry. A wet ball will make length and direction more difficult.

The ideal conditions are when a wicket, which has been wet and soft, is drying out under a hot sun. There is sponginess under a thin surface of hardness. The sponginess helps the spin to bite while the surface hardness gives speed off the pitch. Thus in such conditions spin bowling can be quite unplayable and produce freak disasters for a batting side (recall how England's slow left armer Derek Underwood destroyed the Pakistanis on such a wicket in the Lord's Test of 1974).

Very dry and hard wickets are of no assistance to spin, while soft, damp wickets slow the ball down. Although plenty of turn can still be extracted, the batsman has plenty of time to watch the ball onto his bat.

Off-breaks and leg-breaks
The first thing to learn about off or leg spin is how

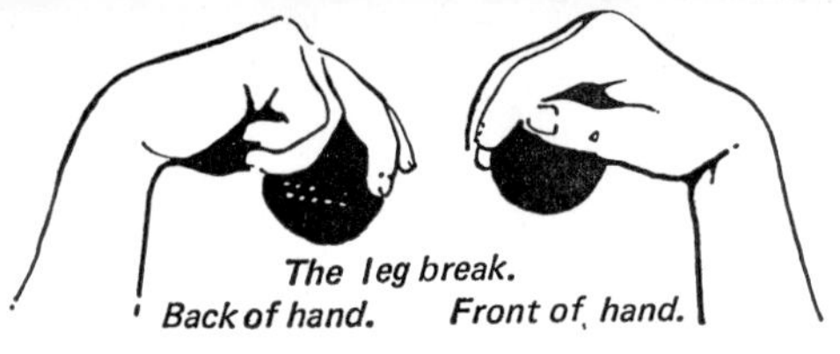

The leg break.
Back of hand.   *Front of hand.*

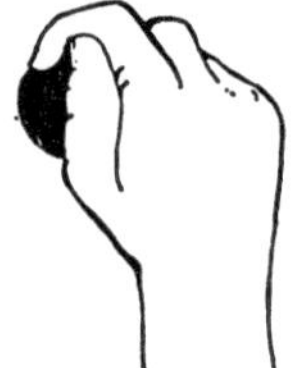

The off break from back of hand.

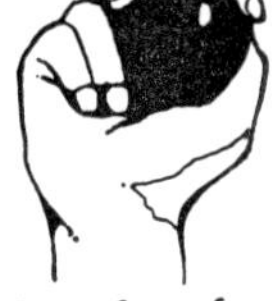

Seen from front of hand.

to grip the ball for it is not, in fact, held tucked in the hand.

The fingers play the all-important part with the principle being to start the ball spinning as it is being tossed forward.

For the off break the common method is for the top joint of the first finger to grip across the seam of the ball (the rough part) and this becomes the main spinning lever.

The second finger, well spaced, also grips across the seam with the thumb lying along the seam.

The spin is given by the wrist being cocked backwards then snapped forward with the first finger dragging sharply downwards and the thumb flipping upwards.

After the ball has been delivered, the hand cuts across the body with the palm pointing upwards.

For the leg break the top joint of the thumb and first two fingers are spaced apart gripping across the seam. The third finger cups the ball and lies along the seam to produce the leg spin.

The wrist is bent inwards and only snaps straight as the ball is delivered. The third and fourth fingers flick upwards and forwards while the thumb side of the hand snaps down. After delivery the hand finishes with the palm upwards.

Swerve

Making the ball swerve and change direction in flight is most common when the new ball is in use.

It is the shiny, polished surface which produces the swerve either from the off or legside and known, respectively, as inswing or outswing.

Most swerve bowlers grip the ball with the seam pointing down the pitch and vertically and lying between the first and second fingers.

The off swerve comes with the arm swung up over the head and away from the body on the downward movement.

For the leg swerve or outswing a slightly round arm swing is employed.

Making the ball swerve, however, is generally regarded as not so much something that can be learnt as a lucky complement to the action of some bowlers over others.

In any event, it depends very largely on the density of the atmosphere. For example, in heavy overcast and sultry weather the swerve can be amazingly pronounced. In clear weather there may be no movement at all. If it is a windy day, the swerve bowler either operates into the wind or with the wind coming from the side where he needs most help for the swerve.

Fast bowling
The fast bowler is sometimes disparagingly referred to as the workhorse of the attack and because of the physical effort he is obliged to put into his action, he operates in fairly short, sharp bursts of a few overs at a time.

Because of the physical effort involved it is important that the fast bowler should not be tired out too soon and one way he can help himself is to perfect an easy rhythmical run-up and delivery. It also has to be an exact run-up since he must land his right foot as far forward as the rules allow without giving away a 'no ball'. The run-up, too, is far from finished with delivery of the ball. The fast bowler must have a follow through of a few paces to guard against any checking of pace.

One point about the follow-through: the bowler should veer slightly away from the wicket otherwise his boots are likely to damage the area just in front of the batting crease. Umpires frequently have to tell fast bowlers about this and if the trouble persists, they can have the bowler taken off for the rest of the innings.

The most effective and spectacular method a fast bowler employs to take his wickets is by bowling his opponents and this is done by sheer speed of delivery, by the 'yorker' which we have discussed earlier, or by an off-break, that is to say the ball that comes back in, probably to clip the off stump.

But whichever method is employed, the ball is bound to bounce over the stumps unless it is well pitched up and here the fast bowler faces the danger of seeing his delivery turned into a score-able half-volley.

Although it is always satisfying to hit the stumps, however, a large proportion of the fast bowler's wickets are achieved by catches behind, taken either by the wicket-keeper or slip fielders.

The balls that produce these wickets are likely to be outswingers. That is to say a ball that pitches on or just outside the off-stump which the batsman is obliged to play. The late swing away to the off finds the edge of the bat . . . and the chorus of 'owzat' goes up.

There is one ball in the fast bowler's armoury not yet touched on . . . the bumper. It may not be quite within the strict spirit of sport, but it is legitimate enough. It happens normally when the bowler attacks the leg stump and allows the odd delivery to be pitched short of length. By a whip-lash delivery he achieves sometimes alarming lift and the wise batsman takes avoiding action by ducking. If, however, he is a compulsive hooker, then he may well give his wicket away by hooking 'down fine leg's throat' or, in other words, lofting a catch.

Remember, bumpers are legitimate 'warfare' but they should be bowled only occasionally otherwise the fast bowler will face a possible charge of intimidation.

One step further from bumpers, by the way, is the beamer and this really will cause a ticking off for the fast bowler. This is a wild full toss aimed at the batsman's head and in the heat of critical Test matches in recent years the odd beamer has been bowled.

The medium-pacer
While the fast bowler operates in short, sharp bursts and the spin bowler may only expect to be employed for long spells if the state of the wicket suits him, the bowler who must bear the brunt of the work is the medium-pacer.

By definition, his is the least exacting technique and therefore he will bowl far more overs in a season on all types of wicket than the others.

And since a straight medium-paced delivery must be a mild affair for the batsman, he has to rely on cunning to collect his wickets.

The first skill he must acquire, however, is complete control of length, direction and pace variety.

It is true that by keeping plugging away on a steady line and length, the medium-pacer may so exasperate the batsman that, in an attempt to get out of a rut, he finally has a wild swing and loses his wicket.

But a medium-pacer has far more subtle methods than that to employ. He can bowl, say, a few balls that pitch on off stump and move away. Then, next delivery, send one down that breaks to leg or goes straight on with the arm. The batsman, lulled into expecting the same as the first few balls, is totally unprepared.

Another method might be to send down three or four balls of varying length but so pitched that the batsman is in no doubt as to whether he should play forward or back. Then he tosses one down on perfect length to leave the batsman in two minds about going forward or back.

It will be seen from all of this that the medium-pacer must be able to employ swerve and spin in addition to maintaining length and direction.

He has to 'think' his opponents out by relying on patience and the knack of knowing when to pop in the unexpected delivery. He should therefore employ a stock ball – that is to say he must concentrate on one particular type of delivery for most of each over and then put in the unexpected ball.

The stock ball is usually the off break, the stock length good and the stock pace medium. It is the odd ball that varies that will get the wickets.

Tip: Watch Tom Cartwright, the veteran Somerset bowler, who is probably the finest exponent of medium-paced bowling in the country.

Slow bowling

The slow bowler, like the medium-pacer, has to be a patient, persevering character, working hard for his wickets unless he happens to find one of those worn or drying pitches where he can expect a rare haul of victims.

And there are other similarities, too. He has to have complete control of length otherwise he will suffer real 'stick' from big-hitting batsmen. Accurate length on the other hand will bring the batsman watchfully forward.

Flight, too, plays an important part in bringing success. By arcing the ball either higher or lower than for the stock delivery, the slow bowler can

lure the batsmen respectively into playing frac-
tionally too late or too early.

Of the two types of delivery which must be
disguised by avoiding any obvious change of
bowling action, the more effective is the slower
ball when the batsman commits himself too soon.
For this reason you will hear a commentator re-
ferring to a slow man bowling 'into the wind'
which obviously helps to accentuate the slower
ball.

As to the most effective ball in the slow
bowler's armoury, the leg break is regarded as the
delivery more likely to do damage. The off
break needs variation of spin, length, width and
pace to achieve much effect. An underpitched
off-break is of no value and obviously any deviation of direction straying to the legside will make
it an easy ball to sweep or glide away.

Leg breaks should be pitched well up on or
just outside the leg stump compelling the batsman to come forward.

They are bowled by turning the wrist with the
back of the hand to the batsman, the ball being
delivered from the little finger side of the hand.
By a very extreme turn of the wrist the googly is
effected – the ball bowled with a leg-break
action but breaking from the off side instead.

How to succeed – try to get the batsman reaching forward without getting to the pitch of the
ball and so bowling him; lure him out in an
attempt to reach the ball before it bounces but
failing to do so; encourage him to hit against the
break at a ball not quite up to him; keep up a
succession of leg breaks on the leg stump, then

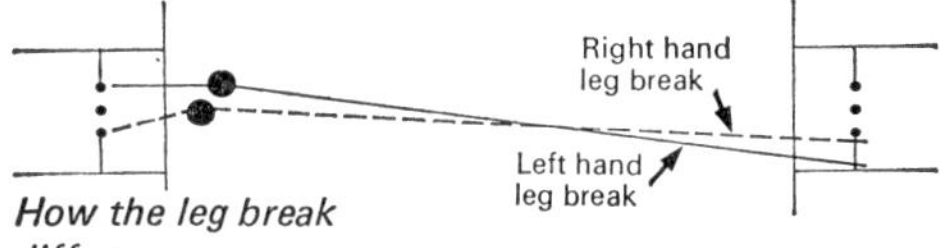

How the leg break differs.

toss down a top-spin or googly pitching on the off stump and hope that the batsman is fooled into believing it is another leg-break.

The slow left-armer

Elsewhere in this handbook, we have dealt with batting and bowling techniques with the right-hander in mind and invited a left-handed player to think in opposite terms. With slow bowling, however, the left-armer is in an exclusive band.

For the leg break, as already mentioned the slow bowler's stock in trade, comes much more easily to the left-armer and can be bowled with greater accuracy of length and direction.

The ball is flighted from the off to the leg then either breaks back from leg or straightens.

The left-armer must create doubt as to the length of the ball. He will use the same arts as the leg breaker, but more flexibility of pace is possible.

Other effective balls he can use include the ball that continues its course from the off after it has pitched – that is, it goes straight on with the arm and is achieved by using no wrist turn in the delivery.

Then there is the occasional ball which pitches outside the off stump and breaks in from the off. This is known as the chinaman.

Tip: Always bowl in such a way that the bats-man can only hit into the offside field. Crowd that side of the wicket with fielders for he will rarely be able to play to leg without risk.

Tips to bowlers

The bowler, sometimes in collaboration with his captain, sometimes without, must decide his own placing of the fielders. The basic field is for an inner ring of fielders and an outer ring for the hard-hit shots and do not be afraid to 'crowd' an incoming batsman – that is to say bring up one or two extra fielders into close catching positions as the new batsman tentatively plays his first few balls.

The bowler can also use some pre-arranged signalling plan to place a fielder in a position towards which he can try to lure the batsman to hit.

Always be on the alert for the caught and bowled chance when completing the follow-through after delivery.

And get sharply behind the stumps to receive the return throw from a fielder when a batsman goes for a run. A run-out may be the result of such quick-thinking.

Do not be reticent about asking for sawdust for the pitch and a towel for the ball when bowling in wet conditions after rain. This avoids the possibility of losing control or even injury to yourself.

One final appeal – for the sake of cricket generally – try to be fairly brisk in bowling your overs. The sluggish over-rate is one of the few but fair complaints made against the game today.

Fielding

Cricket's older generation of enthusiasts are quite critical of what they claim to be the damaging effect of limited-overs cricket on the basic techniques of the game.

Careless shots, bowlers on shortened run-ups, no encouragement for the slow bowler . . . those are just some of the grouses.

But what the diehards cannot deny is that the limited-over game has immensely improved the standard of fielding at all levels of cricket.

The reckless pursuit of runs in the limited over game has sharpened up a side of cricket that was somewhat overlooked in the past. This is a wholly admirable situation since it is fair to say that fielding was once regarded as something of a chore, a necessary evil part of the game if not batting or bowling. Today the top-class cover fielder is a priceless asset in any side.

It is an admirable situation also because an enthusiastic player without any great talent for batting or bowling can come into his own as a fielder just by his very keenness.

The positions

Fielding falls basically into two categories . . . the close catcher and the outfielder and it should become quickly apparent which is the most suitable.

The close catcher obviously has to be quick in reaction and constantly alert; the outfielder must be a fast runner, a good judge of high catches and the possessor of a strong throwing arm.

The close catchers will be primarily positioned in the slips, at short leg, silly mid-off, silly mid-on

The field placings.

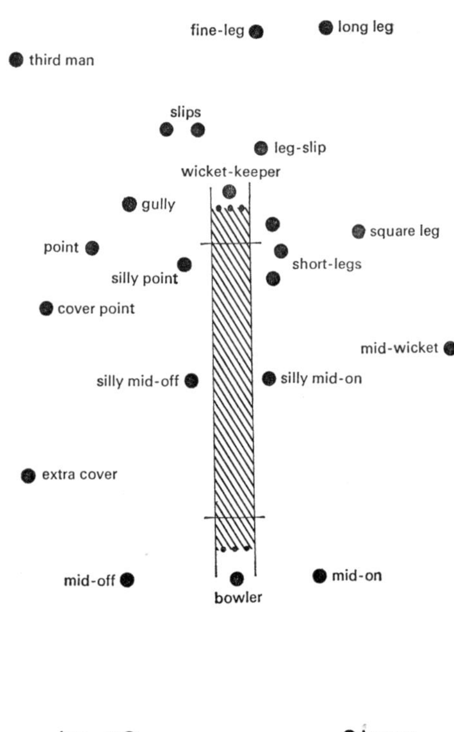

fine-leg
long leg
third man
slips
leg-slip
wicket-keeper
gully
square leg
point
short-legs
silly point
cover point
mid-wicket
silly mid-off
silly mid-on
extra cover
mid-off
mid-on
bowler
long-off
long-on

and point. The outfielder takes up his station in deep positions such as long-on, third man, long-leg, extra cover and deep mid-wicket.

Let us look, though, at some of the key positions starting with cover. This is bound to be an important placing since a steady bowler will pitch the ball on or outside the off stump and most of the batsman's shots will go in cover's direction.

The fielder should be about 20 or 30 yards from the bat and be able to swoop easily on the ball, pick up with either hand and return smart and low over the stumps to the wicket-keeper. Above all cover must be capable of taking really hard-hit catches.

The slips: This is one of the most demanding positions in the field, since, although not much physical exertion is required, the mental concentration is intense. The slip fielder – and often there are as many as three employed – must watch every ball with great care since the batsman is ever likely to snick a sharp chance. This means, of course, that the slip fielder must have fine eyesight and razor-sharp reflexes.

Mid-off: Often this position is occupied by the captain since it is a perfect station from which both to encourage and advise his bowler and also direct field placings. Normally mid-off is about 20–25 yards from the bat and will have a lot of off-drives to deal with. Catches can often come in this direction, too, but in most cases they will be hard-hit chances off the full face of the bat so mid-off will need strong hands.

Third man: Not a catching position, but of

much importance economically. Cuts and edges that elude the slips will all come third man's way and general alertness makes the difference between an easy single and the chance of converting it into a second run. Third man's requirements, therefore, are plenty of speed to cut off boundaries and the ability to pick up on the run and return long throws into the wicket-keeper's gloves.

Mid-on: Although we have dwelt so far with the far more important emphasis laid on fielding in modern cricket, there are still some players who just do not have either the speed of thought or foot to make good fielders, but who are still essential members of the team, more often than not being fast bowlers.

So the captain looks for a place in the field where he can best 'hide' his weak fielder and mid-on is usually deputed. This is because batsmen rarely play shots in this direction. It is far easier to off-drive than to on-drive; likewise a ball on the legside is most usually played square towards mid-wicket or glided behind the wicket.

Alertness

Whether a fielder is in the deep or close in, he must be ready to make the fastest possible move to any ball that comes his way.

For those fielding deep, at cover, mid-off and mid-on, the main task is to stop ground shots and save runs and if they are already moving as the ball is bowled, they will be all the better equipped to do so.

One can easily tell the quality of fielders by noting whether or not they are walking in rather like stalking cats as the bowler starts his run-up.

The close fielders, of course, are not on the move but at the crouch. They must be so positioned that they can catch anything within reach, be the ball above their heads or at their toes.

Therefore they should be neither standing nor settled on their haunches, but be in a crouch and on their toes with their weight evenly divided so that they can move either way should the situation demand.

Throwing

Throwing the ball in is somewhat a matter of muscle — some fielders have powerful, long throws; for those, however, who cannot propel the ball great distances the basic art of throwing can still be followed with reasonable satisfaction.

First, always aim for the wicket-keeper's end unless there is a real chance of a run out with a fast return to the bowler.

Try to achieve a full toss straight into the keeper's gloves aiming at a point a few inches above the stumps (the keeper will always acknowledge such a return with the raising of his gloved hand after a sweep of his arms over the stumps).

If the thrower is not strong enough to achieve a full toss he should try to send a long-hop into the keeper's gloves. Any ball that pitches round about the 'keeper's feet is a bad return since, if a run-out chance is there, he cannot quickly sweep off the bails.

Remember to try and avoid returning the ball to the bowler's end unless absolutely necessary. The bowler is one of the team's assets and he does not want to risk injury to his hands in trying to take a hot throw on the full toss or pitching unpleasantly near his feet. Indeed, the bowler will even let the ball escape his grasp if he thinks there is any danger of injury.

The possibility of the bowler allowing the ball to pass him, incidentally, brings to bear the important, if elementary, aspect of backing up.

This means that whenever a fielder returns the ball, one or more fielders behind the wicket-keeper and in line with the throw should be on the alert to cut off an overthrow.

A keen fielding side should not be guilty of such error which only makes a side look lazy and undisciplined.

Catching

The most important aspect of fielding comes down to the ability to hold catches. As the adage has it 'catches win matches'.

The fielder has two types of catching to learn — the close catch taken near the bat and the lengthy, judged catch.

Slip fielding, of course, offers most of the close catching chances and it is important, by determining on the pace of the bowler and wicket, the correct distance to stand back from the wicket. There is a difference of opinion on whether the slip should watch ball or bat, but at least all are agreed that as the ball arrives, the fingers of the hand will be turned towards the ground and

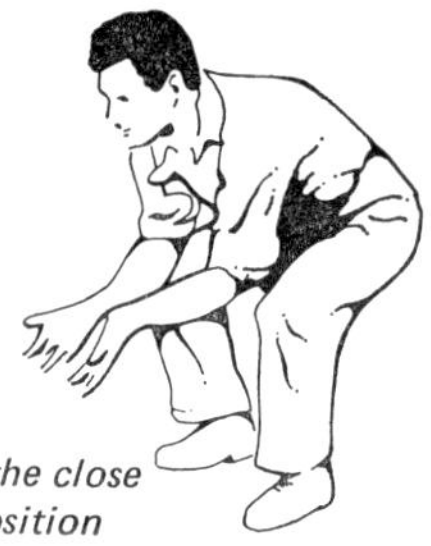

Fielding: the close catching position

Outfielding: preparing for taking a catch.

ready to yield under the impact. The harder the catch, the more the hands must yield.

The judged catch is that in which the outfielder has the time to assess the flight of the ball.

It is no use for the fielder to move from his position until he has decided where the catch is going. Too often a fielder runs in too soon and then discovers that the ball is going to sail over his head.

Having assessed the flight, the catcher should try and cover the required ground before preparing to make the catch. A ball taken on the run may look spectacular but there is also a high element of risk that the ball may bounce out of the hands because the catcher is not correctly balanced.

Although fielders vary in their favourite method of actually holding the catch (close to the body, close to the ground, at arms' length), they should all attempt to take the ball as near to eye level as possible.

If the catch is taken below eye level, the ball cannot be watched during the last second.

It is also difficult to form cupped hands for a high catch unless the fingers are in an upwards direction and obviously this is impossible if the hands are held low. So, even if taking a low catch, the knees should be bent and the hands on a level with the eyes.

Above all else, catching requires regular practice. There is no better way than for a group of players to get together and take it in turns with a bat to loft and hit catches to their colleagues.

Wicket-keeping

Wicket-keeping equipment
No wicket-keeper can hope to do himself justice unless his equipment – gloves and pads – are adequate.

The keeper should aim to wear gloves that are large enough to allow at least one pair of inner gloves which should fit the hand loosely. These inners must also be big enough to take extra padding in the general protection of the hands.

But the amount of padding inside the gloves should not be such that the keeper is unable to get a good feel of the ball.

The outer gloves need plenty of attention or else they will become hard and slippery. Eucalyptus or saddler's soap will keep the leather in good condition and a little resin will provide the desired slightly sticky effect. But do not overdo this preparation or else the ball will become sticky which will hardly please bowlers.

The pads should be sturdy and fairly wide. They are much larger than the pads worn by batsmen and consequently quite unsuitable for running.

Remember that pads are primarily for protection – a good wicket-keeper will not deign to use his pads to stop the ball unless absolutely necessary.

Standing up
The wicket-keeper should always get as good a sight of the ball as possible, never allowing the batsman to impede his view.

He should squat on the offside of the wicket with the left toe in line with the off stump about

eighteen inches behind.

As the bowler begins his run-up, the keeper's hands should be on the ground with the palms upwards and the arms between the knees and with the heels on the ground. This latter position takes into account that the keeper is the busiest man in the fielding side and cannot be expected to be on his toes all the time.

However, as he prepares to receive the ball, the weight is transferred from the heels to the toes as he moves from the squat to the crouch to receive the ball. Remember to rise after the ball has pitched – it is useless to get up too early

Every ball should be taken in both hands unless a ball is so wide of the wicket that the keeper has to dive left or right. The fingers should be pointed towards the ground with hands together and palms facing the bowler.

The hands, too, should never be moved forward to take the ball as if to snatch at it. Always allow it to come into the cupped hands in its own time. And allow the hands to yield a little upon impact.

The body should be close behind the hands but if the ball is at all wide move only the right foot to deliveries wide of the off stump or the left foot to balls on the legside. But while it is acceptable to move sideways, never step backwards to receive the ball.

Standing back

At early schools level of cricket it is sometimes considered 'cissy' to stand well back to fast bowling, but this is a fallacy.

For one thing, if the keeper stands too far up in an ill-advised show of bravado he may well suffer injury and with the keeper out of action a fielding side is badly handicapped.

For another, the keeper is far more effective if he does stand well back to fast bowling. Do not go in for half measures — stand far enough back to take the ball on the long hop or, in other words, at a comfortable height.

A stumping chance is obviously virtually impossible, but there are plenty of opportunities for edged catches.

If the batsman strikes the ball, however, always run up to the wicket to receive the returned ball from the fielder, taking the ball behind the stumps.

One debatable point in standing back is the question of whether, if the ball flies off the edge of the bat, the keeper should dive across his first slip fielder in an attempt to take the catch himself. Top-class keepers like Kent's Alan Knott tend to do this. It is inadvisable for the more humble of keepers since he will most likely miss the catch that might have been a comfortable chance to the slip.

Catching
Once the wicket-keeper has mastered the art of taking everything cleanly in two hands, he should be capable of taking most of the catches that come his way, especially when he is standing up to the slow and medium-pace bowlers.

This is because the ball that comes off the edge of the bat will not really deviate at all until it has landed in the gloves. Consequently the keeper does not need to move his hands at all when he hears the snick.

When standing back to the fast bowler, how-ever, he has a fraction more time before the ball is in his gloves and if he hears a snick there must be a temptation to move the hands forward in anti-cipation. Don't.

The keeper, too, should be the only fielder to appeal when he makes what he thinks is a catch. Yet so often all the slips will throw up their hands in a loud chorus the instant they hear the snick and can quite often panic the keeper into snatch-ing too soon and dropping the ball.

Stumping and running out
One exercise the wicket-keeper should under-take on receiving the ball is to sweep his gloves over the top of the wicket. He does this in case

there could be a chance of stumping the bats-man.

Successful stumping requires high speed so, for a start, one foot should always be near the stumps. But again do not snatch at the ball and remember above all that the ball cannot be taken from in front of the wicket.

The likeliest stumping chances come from slow bowling and the keeper should always watch the bowler's hand at the point of delivery to see what sort of ball he intends to bowl. Often slow bowlers and keepers operate a secret signalling code to determine the next delivery in mind.

Leg breaks tend to reap most stumping chances and the ball that turns to leg is rather more difficult to turn into a stumping.

Efficient running out requires the keeper to remember to gather the fielder's throw cleanly first before breaking the wicket. He should stand behind the stumps and be facing the fielder. He will also have to be agile since some throws will return so high he will have to leap like a goalkeeper; others will be so low he will try to gather on the half-volley.

Captaincy

Selecting your side

The qualifications for captaining a cricket team do not necessarily include being the best player. Instead, the captain must be a natural leader, capable of handling people, of setting an example by enthusiasm and alertness in the field, a psychologist inasmuch as he must be able to handle the temperaments of individual team members and be a tactician.

In the selection of his side he should aim at fielding four recognised bowlers and at least two all-rounders (players who can both bat and bowl to a fair degree of efficiency).

His bowling strength is ideally made up of the front-line assault from two opening fast bowlers with a couple of medium-pacers as his first change bowlers, with a slow bowler – most preferably a left-arm leg break specialist – completing the attack.

(In current first-class cricket, with its increased numbers of trophies and money at stake than ever before, there is a rather regrettable tendency today to omit or economise on spin bowling because it can sometimes prove an expensive luxury with runs being scored quicker.)

The captain's batting line-up begins with his opening pair whose task it is to 'see off' the new ball attack, making life that bit easier for the specialist batsmen to follow.

The ideal opening partnership is between one batsman who can get runs and the other who can play a sheet anchor role and remain at the wicket for a fair time even though he may not be making much contribution to the scoring.

Batsmen 3 to 6 should be the stroke players of the side. Next, it is useful, particularly with today's propensity for limited overs cricket, to have at least one blacksmith-type batsman, that is to say a slogger of the ball.

The tail of the batting order comprises the 'rabbits' – usually the pace bowlers with no pretensions to batting.

The wicket-keeper has as yet been unmentioned. He may, indeed, be a batsman and if he is capable of opening the innings that is all to the good. If the opposing side have batted first, no one will be more aware of the pace of the wicket than the keeper.

But if the keeper cannot bat, but is a first-class operator behind the stumps, then it matters not if he goes in at No 11 – his value will still be inestimable in the field.

Exploiting the elements

The captain must have a sound knowledge of the many quirks of cricket in this country and one essential is an awareness of how the weather may affect a match.

So, having won the toss, he must have a good look at the wicket before deciding whether to bat or insert the opposition.

If the pitch is heavy and sodden – a dead wicket – he should elect to bat first for there will be little or no pace in it and the batsmen will have all the time in the world to play the ball.

If the weather, rather than the pitch, is heavy and humid, he fields first provided he has the fast bowlers who can make the ball swing and swerve in the atmosphere.

If hot sun has replaced recent rain then the wicket may well prove to be a sticky one in which case he will again field if he has the spinners to exploit the conditions.

And if the wicket is hard he will probably bat unless he has prior knowledge that the wicket plays very fast. In this latter case he might want his own batsmen to field first so that they have the advantage of judging the pace of the wicket for themselves.

Should the captain lose the toss then there is still a decision to take. For the captain of the side batting second has the choice of using the light or heavy roller on the wicket between innings.

He calls for the light roller if the wicket is dry, but in danger of breaking up; a soft wicket should be treated with the heavy roller because it will make a damp surface relatively mild in the early part of the innings, the moisture having been forced up to the surface.

Batting and declarations
In the introduction to captaincy, mention was made of the captain's need to be something of a psychologist in the handling of his side.

It applies both to his bowlers and batsmen. A bad captain is one who orders his batsmen to take up tactics totally alien to their normal styles.

Particularly in lower levels of cricket captains order batsmen to hit or keep the score moving and this may well lead to their swinging at everything and getting themselves out unnecessarily.

Conversely, if told to stay there, they may become so intent on stonewall resistance that no runs accrue at all.

Except in the most extremely tight situations of trying to snatch a dramatic victory or struggling to save a match, the captain should only tell his batsmen to carry on in their normal style.

Continuing the theme of the captain's role in his side's innings, we come to the question of declarations for which no hard and fast rules apply except to say that he should never leave a declaration so late that the opposition have not even a sporting chance of achieving their set target.

Bowling and field placing

Bowlers are a breed of player far more given to temperament than batsmen. Perhaps this is because of the great physical or mental strain imposed upon them, perhaps because a man who hits a hundred is likely to achieve far more acclaim than the bowler who takes five, six or seven wickets in an innings.

For whatever reason, however, the captain handles his bowlers with care and consideration.

Some bowlers can bowl on for long spells, others prefer to operate in short bursts. The captain must know all about his men and be able to spot when a bowler is tiring.

Obviously if the state of the pitch is to a bowler's liking and he is taking wickets then his tail will be up and he will be able to bowl for a much longer spell.

But if there is little in the pitch, then it is good

practice constantly to ring the changes. The batsmen are then put on their guard because they keep facing fresh bowlers with different actions.

In compliance with his bowlers' wishes, the captain must always be ready to vary his field placings. If a bowler is being hit then the captain must try to plug the gaps; if a wicket falls he must call in extra close fielders to crowd the new batsman.

The structure of cricket

All cricket in England — from Test level to the village and school game — comes under the embracing umbrella of the Cricket Council.

Until 1966 and the formation by the Government of the Sports Council, the unofficial responsibility for the running of the game belonged to MCC — the Marylebone Cricket Club.

MCC had been formed in 1787 with one Thomas Lord providing his ground in Dorset Fields, St Marylebone ... and whose name is immortalised by Lord's Cricket Ground.

When the Sports Council was introduced in 1966 it asked MCC to set up an official body since it could not deal with a private club. Hence the Cricket Council.

It has three main departments — the Test and County Cricket Board, MCC itself and the National Cricket Association.

The TCCB is in control of all Test matches and first-class cricket in the country, all overseas tours, all the knockout and league competitions and the Minor Counties competition.

MCC, centred at Lord's, the headquarters of the game, is responsible for any changes in the laws, in conjunction with all the overseas countries.

The NCA covers what the TCCB does not — cricket in schools, the services, the women's game and at club level.

Test cricket

The previous page dealt with the structure of cricket in this country, but on a world-wide scale the game comes under the auspices of the International Cricket Conference which was founded in 1909.

Test matches are played between the full members of the ICC – England, Australia, India, West Indies, New Zealand and Pakistan.

(When South Africa withdrew from the British Commonwealth she ceased to become a full member, but under changing rules she is eligible today for re-election).

The first Test was between Australia and England at Melbourne in 1877.

Tests are played in series (normally of five matches), one country touring another, the rota for tours being arranged by the ICC.

The Tests are usually of five days' duration and laws are more or less the same as in English first-class cricket, although there are some slight differences – in Australia and New Zealand, for instance, the bowler's over consists of eight deliveries instead of the six in the English game.

The most famous Test series is that played between England and Australia and is known as the fight for the Ashes.

Two circumstances brought about the origin of the Ashes. In 1882 Australia beat England at The Oval and an obituary appeared in a sporting publication the following day stating 'In affectionate remembrance of English Cricket which died at The Oval 29 August 1882, deeply lamented by a large circle of sorrowing friends and acquaintances RIP. NB: the body will be cremated and the Ashes taken to Australia.'

A year later an England team in Australia won a Test series and some ladies burnt a bail after the final Test, placed the Ashes in a small urn and presented it to England's captain, The Hon. Ivo Bligh.

These Ashes were later given to MCC and are kept permanently at Lord's.

England v. Australia

The Ashes

The results of matches between England and Australia are as follows:

Season	Captains England	Australia
1876–77	James Lillywhite	D. W. Gregory
1878–79	Lord Harris	D. W. Gregory
1880	Lord Harris	W. L. Murdoch
1881–82	A. Shaw	W. L. Murdoch
1882	A. N. Hornby	W. L. Murdoch
1882–83	Hon. Ivo Bligh	W. L. Murdoch
1884	Lord Harris	W. L. Murdoch
1884–85	A. Shrewsbury	T. Horan
1886	A. G. Steel	H. J. H. Scott
1886–87	A. Shrewsbury	P. S. McDonnell
1887–88	W. W. Read	P. S. McDonnell
1888	W. G. Grace	P. S. McDonnell
1890	W. G. Grace	W. L. Murdoch
1891–92	W. G. Grace	J. M. Blackham
1893	W. G. Grace	J. M. Blackham
1894–95	A. E. Stoddart	G. Giffen
1896	W. G. Grace	G. H. S. Trott
1897–98	A. E. Stoddart	G. H. S. Trott
1899	A. C. MacLaren	J. Darling
1901–02	A. C. MacLaren	J. Darling
1902	A. C. MacLaren	J. Darling
1903–04	P. F. Warner	M. A. Noble
1905	Hon. F. S. Jackson	J. Darling
1907–08	A. O. Jones	M. A. Noble
1909	A. C. MacLaren	M. A. Noble
1911–12	J. W. H. T. Douglas	C. Hill
1912	C. B. Fry	S. E. Gregory
1920–21	J. W. H. T. Douglas	W. W. Armstrong
1921	Hon. L. H. Tennyson	W. W. Armstrong

Season	Tests	Won by England	Won by Australia	Drawn
1876–77	2	1	1	0
1878–79	1	0	1	0
1880	1	1	0	0
1881–82	4	0	2	2
1882	1	0	1	0
1882–83	4	2	2	0
1884	3	1	0	2
1884–85	5	3	2	0
1886	3	3	0	0
1886–87	2	2	0	0
1887–88	1	1	0	0
1888	3	2	1	0
1890	2	2	0	0
1891–92	3	1	2	0
1893	3	1	0	2
1894–95	5	3	2	0
1896	3	2	1	0
1897–98	5	1	4	0
1899	5	0	1	4
1901–02	5	1	4	0
1902	5	1	2	2
1903–04	5	3	2	0
1905	5	2	0	3
1907–08	5	1	4	0
1909	5	1	2	2
1911–12	5	4	1	0
1912	3	1	0	2
1920–21	5	0	5	0
1921	5	0	3	2

The Ashes (continued)

Captains

Season	England	Australia
1924–25	A. E. R. Gilligan	H. L. Collins
1926	A. W. Carr	H. L. Collins
1928–29	A. P. F. Chapman	J. Ryder
1930	A. P. F. Chapman	W. M. Woodfull
1932–33	D. R. Jardine	W. M. Woodfull
1934	R. E. S. Wyatt	W. M. Woodfull
1936–37	G. O. Allen	D. G. Bradman
1938	W. R. Hammond	D. G. Bradman
1946–47	W. R. Hammond	D. G. Bradman
1948	N. W. D. Yardley	D G. Bradman
1950–51	F. R. Brown	A. L. Hassett
1953	L. Hutton	A. L. Hassett
1954–55	L. Hutton	I. W. Johnson
1956	P. B. H. May	I. W. Johnson
1958–59	P. B. H. May	R. Benaud
1961	P. B. H. May	R. Benaud
1962–63	E. R. Dexter	R. Benaud
1964	E. R. Dexter	R. B. Simpson
1965–66	M. J. K. Smith	R. B. Simpson
1968	M. C. Cowdrey	W. M. Lawry
1970–71	R. Illingworth	W. M. Lawry
1972	R. Illingworth	I. M. Chappell
1974–75	M. H. Denness	I. M. Chappell

In Australia . . . .

In England . . . .

Totals . . . .

Season	Tests	Won by England	Won by Australia	Drawn
1924–25	5	1	4	0
1926	5	1	0	4
1928–29	5	4	1	0
1930	5	1	2	2
1932–33	5	4	1	0
1934	5	1	2	2
1936–37	5	2	3	0
1938	4	1	1	2
1946–47	5	0	3	2
1948	5	0	4	1
1950–51	5	1	4	0
1953	5	1	0	4
1954–55	5	3	1	1
1956	5	2	1	2
1958–59	5	0	4	1
1961	5	1	2	2
1962–63	5	1	1	3
1964	5	0	1	4
1965–66	5	1	1	3
1968	5	1	1	3
1970–71	6	2	0	4
1972	5	2	2	1
1974–75	6	1	4	1
	119	43	59	17
	101	28	27	46
	220	71	86	63

England v. West Indies

The Wisden Trophy

The results of matches between England and the West Indies are as follows:

	Captains	
Season	England	West Indies
1928	A. P. F. Chapman	R. K. Nunes
1929–30	Hon F. S. G. Calthorpe	E. L. G. Hoad
1933	D. R. Jardine	G. C. Grant
1934–35	R. E. S. Wyatt	G. C. Grant
1939	W. R. Hammond	R. S. Grant
1947–48	G. O. Allen	J. D. C. Goddard
1950	N. W. D. Yardley	J. D. C. Goddard
1953–54	L. Hutton	J. B. Stollmeyer
1957	P. B. H. May	J. D. C. Goddard
1959–60	P. B. H. May	F. C. M. Alexander
1963	E. R. Dexter	F. M. Worrell
1966	M. C. Cowdrey	G. S. Sobers
1967–68	M. C. Cowdrey	G. S. Sobers
1969	R. Illingworth	G. S. Sobers
1973	R. Illingworth	R. B. Kanhai
1973–74	M. Denness	R. B. Kanhai

In England ....
In West Indies ....
Totals ....

Season	Tests	Won by England	Won by W. Indies	Drawn
1928	3	3	0	0
1929–30	4	1	1	2
1933	3	2	0	1
1934–35	4	1	2	1
1939	3	1	0	2
1947–48	4	0	2	2
1950	4	1	3	0
1953–54	5	2	2	1
1957	5	3	0	2
1959–60	5	1	0	4
1963	5	1	3	1
1966	5	1	3	1
1967–68	5	1	0	4
1969	3	2	0	1
1973	3	0	2	1
1973–74	5	1	1	3
	34	14	11	9
	32	7	8	17
	66	21	19	26

England and the 1974 Test Matches

After salvaging England's reputation in the West Indies by winning the final Test, Mike Denness of Kent led England through a relatively easy run-in to the 1974 international season.

England, hardly raising a sweat, won all three Tests against the Indians, but then found the going – and the weather – very much tougher against Pakistan.

Aided by the wet weather which did so much to wreck the 1974 season, England drew all three Tests with Pakistan, and only a slow innings by Keith Fletcher prevented the Tourists from winning the final Test at the Oval.

The rout of the Indians began at Old Trafford with a 113-run victory, a match in which two English batsmen scored centuries – Keith Fletcher (123) and John Edrich (100).

At Lord's, in the Second Test, England's victory was even more decisive.

This time they won by an innings and 285 runs – and with three centuries.

Dennis Amiss scored 188, skipper Denness hit 118 and Tony Greig added 106 in a mammoth first innings total of 629.

At Edgbaston, the winning margin was almost as big – an innings and 78 runs as England completed a whitewash over the clearly outclassed Indians.

David Lloyd was the chief wrecker of the Indian bowling on this occasion – he scored an undefeated 214 as England climbed to 459 for two declared. And Denness added to his growing stature by scoring 100.

The runs, however, were very much more difficult to come by against Pakistan.

Rain prevented a result in the opening Test – and probably robbed England of victory in spite of a very shaky start. They were skittled out for 183 in their first innings, but hit back with 238 for six in the second – against Pakistan's two innings' total of 464 – and were within 44 runs of winning when rain washed out the final day's play at Headingley.

The Second Test was also ruined by rain – at Lord's – but England looked to be in real danger of surrendering their unbeaten record in the deciding Test at the Oval.

Pakistan scored 600 for 7 declared in their first innings, but as they had taken two days to do it the chances of a result were clearly remote.

England avoided the follow on by scoring 545, and Pakistan were 94 for 4 when the game closed.

Summing up, 1974 will never be remembered as a vintage year – certainly not as far as the weather is concerned – and the matches against Pakistan were particularly unsatisfactory.

But it was a year in which Mike Denness appeared to consolidate his position as England's skipper and to prepare himself for the battle of the Ashes in Australia.

1974 Test Match averages

England v. India
England – Batting

	I	NO	R	H'est	Avge
D. Lloyd	2	1	260	214*	260·00
K. W. R. Fletcher	3	2	189	123*	189·00
J. H. Edrich	3	1	203	100*	101·50
M. H. Denness	4	1	289	118	96·33
D. L. Amiss	4	0	370	188	92·50
A. W. Greig	2	0	159	106	79·50
R. G. D. Willis	1	0	24	24	24·00
A. P. E. Knott	2	0	26	26	13·00
D. L. Underwood	3	0	25	9	8·33
G. Boycott	2	0	16	10	8·00
C. M. Old	2	0	15	12	7·50
G. G. Arnold	1	0	5	5	5·00

Also batted: M. Hendrick 1-1-1-1*.
* not out.

Bowling

	O	M	R	W	Avge
Old	89	19	249	18	13·83
Hendrick	85	14	215	14	15·35
Willis	36	8	97	5	19·40
Arnold	65·5	13	204	10	20·40
Greig	70·1	16	176	6	29·33
Underwood	67	25	146	4	36·50

Also bowled: Lloyd 2-0-4-0.

India – Batting

	I	NO	R	H'est	Avge
S. S. Naik	2	0	81	77	40·50
F. M. Engineer	6	1	195	86	39·00
S. Gavaskar	6	0	217	101	36·16
G. R. Viswanath	6	0	200	52	33·33

A. V. Mankad	......	2	0	57	43	28·50
E. D. Solkar	....	6	1	98	43	19·60
S. Abid Ali	....	6	0	101	71	16·83
A. L. Wadekar	......	6	0	82	36	13·66
S. Venkataraghavan	..	4	1	13	5*	4·33
B. S. Bedi	....	6	1	15	14	3·00
S. Dadan Lal	......	4	0	11	7	2·75
P. B. Patel	....	4	0	10	5	2·50
E. A. S. Prasanna	....	4	0	9	5	2·25

* not out.

Bowling

		O	M	R	W	Avge
Abid	....	81·3	12	252	6	42·00
Bedi	....	172·2	28	523	10	52·30
Chandrasekhar	....	42	7	126	2	63·00
Prasanna	....	86	10	267	3	89·00
Lal	....	73	19	188	2	94·00
Solkar	....	44	11	125	1	125·00

Also bowled: Venkataraghavan 37-3-96-0.

1974 Test Match averages

England v. Pakistan
England – Batting

	I	NO	R	H'est	Av
K. W. Fletcher	4	1	208	122	69·33
D. L. Amiss	5	1	220	185	55·00
C. M. Old	4	1	116	65	38·66
J. H. Edrich	4	0	144	70	36·00
A. P. E. Knott	4	0	132	83	33·00
D. Underwood	3	1	64	43	32·00
D. Lloyd	5	1	96	48	24·00
M. H. Denness	4	0	91	44	22·75
A. W. Greig	4	0	90	37	22·50
M. Hendrick	2	1	7	6	7·00
G. Arnold	3	0	13	10	4·33
R. G. D. Wills	1	1	1	1*	—

* not out

Bowling	O	M	R	W	Av
Underwood	113·5	48	218	17	12·82
Greig	79·5	23	222	8	27·75
Arnold	121	28	300	10	30·00
Hendrick	63	16	195	6	32·50
Old	88·3	8	324	7	46·28
Willis	35	4	129	2	64·50

Also bowled: Lloyd 2-0-13-0

Pakistan – Batting

	I	NO	R	H'est	Av
Zaheer Abbas	6	0	324	240	54·00
Wasim Raja	4	1	135	53	45·00
Majid Khan	6	0	262	98	43·66
Mushtaq Mohammad	6	0	209	76	34·83
Sadiq Mohammad	6	0	148	43	24·66
Sarfraz Nawaz	5	2	70	53	23·33

	I	NO	R	H'est	Av
Imran Khan	6	1	92	31	18·40
Intikhab Alam	5	1	50	32*	12·50
Shafiq Ahmed	2	0	25	18	12·50
Asif Iqbal	5	0	53	29	10·60
Wasim Bari	4	0	10	4	2·50
Asif Masood	3	3	23	17*	—

* not out.

Bowling

	O	M	R	W	Av
Sarfraz Nawaz	121	34	259	9	28·77
Intikhab Alam	98·4	25	235	8	29·37
Asif Masood ..	104	28	235	7	33·57
Asif Iqbal	16	4	34	1	34·00
Mushtaq Mohammad	41	17	75	2	37·50
Imran Khan ..	112	26	258	5	51·60
Wasim Raja ..	25	6	76	1	76·00
Majid Khan ..	2	0	10	0	—

The County championship

Seventeen counties — including one from Wales Glamorgan — comprise the County Championship which has been in existence since 1864, when Surrey first won the title.

They are, in alphabetical order: Derbyshire, Essex, Glamorgan, Gloucestershire, Hampshire, Kent, Lancashire, Leicestershire, Middlesex, Northamptonshire, Nottinghamshire, Somerset, Surrey, Sussex, Warwickshire, Worcestershire and Yorkshire.

Over the years the rules have regularly been revised and with the introduction of the limited overs game in the 1960s, the Championship has been much reduced in content to allow time to be put aside for the other competitions.

(It is a situation which the diehards deplore since this competition is regarded as the genuine article of cricket and from the individual performances in it the England Test team is selected).

Today each county plays 20 matches — one against each of the others, and, unsatisfactorily, a return fixture against only four of them.

Matches are of three days' duration with 10 points for a win and five each in the rare event of a tie. In addition there is a maximum of eight bonus points for batting and bowling in the first innings only.

A batting point is earned when the total reaches 150, 200, 250 and 300; a bowling point is for every two wickets taken after the first two and within 100 overs.

Also in the first innings only the side batting first is allowed only 100 overs and if they are dismissed within this distance the surplus overs are added to the 100 allowed to the team batting second.

It may all sound complicated and this is the criticism of the thousands who stay away and leave grounds regrettably empty of spectators at Championship fixtures. But it is the Championship title which first-class cricketers covet most and – apart from Test matches – it is the only type of cricket where you will see the first-class game correctly played.

Champion county since 1864

1864	Surrey	1893	Yorkshire
1865	Nottinghamshire	1894	Surrey
1866	Middlesex	1895	Surrey
1867	Yorkshire	1896	Yorkshire
1868	Nottinghamshire	1897	Lancashire
1869	{ Nottinghamshire / Yorkshire	1898	Yorkshire
		1899	Surrey
1870	Yorkshire	1900	Yorkshire
1871	Nottinghamshire	1901	Yorkshire
1872	Nottinghamshire	1902	Yorkshire
1873	{ Gloucestershire / Nottinghamshire	1903	Middlesex
		1904	Lancashire
1874	Gloucestershire	1905	Yorkshire
1875	Nottinghamshire	1906	Kent
1876	Gloucestershire	1907	Notts
1877	Gloucestershire	1908	Yorkshire
1878	Undecided	1909	Kent
1879	{ Nottinghamshire / Lancashire	1910	Kent
		1911	Warwicks
1880	Nottinghamshire	1912	Yorkshire
1881	Lancashire	1913	Kent
1882	{ Nottinghamshire / Lancashire	1914	Surrey
		1919	Yorkshire
1883	Nottinghamshire	1920	Middlesex
1884	Nottinghamshire	1921	Middlesex
1885	Nottinghamshire	1922	Yorkshire
1886	Nottinghamshire	1923	Yorkshire
1887	Surrey	1924	Yorkshire
1888	Surrey	1925	Yorkshire
1889	{ Surrey / Lancashire / Nottinghamshire	1926	Lancashire
		1927	Lancashire
		1928	Lancashire
1890	Surrey	1929	Notts
1891	Surrey	1930	Lancashire
1892	Surrey	1931	Yorkshire

1932	Yorkshire	1956	Surrey
1933	Yorkshire	1957	Surrey
1934	Lancashire	1958	Surrey
1935	Yorkshire	1959	Yorkshire
1936	Derbyshire	1960	Yorkshire
1937	Yorkshire	1961	Hampshire
1938	Yorkshire	1962	Yorkshire
1939	Yorkshire	1963	Yorkshire
1946	Yorkshire	1964	Worcestershire
1947	Middlesex	1965	Worcestershire
1948	Glamorgan	1966	Yorkshire
1949	Middlesex / Yorkshire	1967	Yorkshire
1950	Lancashire / Surrey	1968	Yorkshire
1951	Warwickshire	1969	Glamorgan
1952	Surrey	1970	Kent
1953	Surrey	1971	Surrey
1954	Surrey	1972	Warwickshire
1955	Surrey	1973	Hampshire
		1974	Worcestershire

The 1974 County Championship

The weather, rather than any batting or bowling performances by individuals or teams, decided the 1974 County Championship and produced a somewhat unsatisfactory end to the season.

In the end, Worcestershire won the title by two points from Hampshire on a wet day early in September when neither team played a ball.

Rain washed out play in Worcestershire's match against Essex at Chelmsford and also ended all hope of action in the Hampshire–Yorkshire game at Bournemouth.

So much might have happened in either of those games, but it didn't and Worcestershire were left with a two point advantage with Hampshire unable to do a thing about it.

Many people might consider winning a title in that manner a shade lucky, but not Worcestershire's skipper, Norman Gifford.

He summed up his team's triumph with these words: 'We haven't been lucky. When you play twenty matches over a season, you have to look at the weather situation overall.

'We have had our wet days as well as Hampshire. But this team has shown great character and lifted itself off the floor after taking a terrible hiding in an innings defeat against Hampshire who were then 30 points ahead of us.'

The weather in fact robbed Hampshire of their second successive county championship victory, and for Worcestershire it was their first triumph since 1965.

1974 County Championship Table

		P	W	L	D	Tie	N.R	Bonus Pts.		Pts.
								Bt	Bw	
1	Worcestershire (6)	20	11	3	6	0	0	45	72	227
2	Hampshire (1) ..	20	10	3	6	0	1	55	70	225
3	Northants (3) ..	20	9	2	9	0	0	46	67	203
4	Leicestershire (9)	20	7	7	6	0	0	47	69	186
5	Somerset (10) ..	20	6	4	10	0	0	49	72	181
6	Middlesex (13)..	20	7	5	8	0	0	45	56	171
	Surrey (2)	20	6	4	10	0	0	42	69	171
8	Lancashire (9) ..	20	5	0	15	0	0	47	66	163
9	Warwickshire (7)	20	5	5	10	0	0	44	65	159
10	Kent (4)	20	5	8	7	0	0	33	63	146
	Yorkshire (14) ..	20	4	7	8	0	1	37	69	146
12	Essex (8)	20	4	3	12	1	0	45	51	141
13	Sussex (15)	20	4	9	6	1	0	29	63	137
14	Gloucestershire (5)	19	4	9	6	0	0	29	55	124
15	Notts (17)......	20	1	9	10	0	0	42	66	118
16	Glamorgan (11)	19	2	7	10	0	0	28	56	104
17	Derbyshire (16)	20	1	6	13	0	0	23	62	95

1973 positions in brackets.

Limited overs cricket

Although the limited overs game has captivated a large audience of cricket fans once thought lost to the game, it must be accepted by the keen student that he will see much that does not belong in the text book as players sometimes abandon what they have been taught in the hectic pursuit of success.

That said, cricket is still greatly indebted to the limited overs game for reviving its fortunes.

The Gillette Cup was the first competition to be launched in 1963. It is a knockout tournament between the 17 counties and the five leading teams in the previous season's Minor Counties table.

Matches are of 60 overs a side – each bowler being limited to an allocation of 12 overs – the Cup Final being played on the first Saturday in September at Lord's . . . always a major event in the cricket calendar which attracts a capacity crowd.

The Benson and Hedges Cup is the youngest knockout competition, having been launched in 1972. This is of 55 overs a side (bowlers 11 overs each).

It differs from the Gillette in that the counties plus three sides drawn from the Minor Counties and universities are divided into four zones and play each other on a league basis. The two top teams in each section go forward to the quarter finals whence the competition is played as a knock-out event with the final at Lord's on an early Saturday in July.

The third limited overs contest is the John Player Sunday League in which the 17 counties play each other once, the winners of each match gaining 4 points.

Matches are limited to 40 overs each (play does not start until 2 pm) with the bowlers limited to eight overs each with run-ups to the wicket not exceeding 15 yards.

It is clear, then, that this is the most contrived form of limited overs cricket, but these Sunday afternoon League games attract large crowds and the competition, which began in 1969, has, for many families, replaced a drive in the car or a trip to the seaside as a top Sunday afternoon outing.

The Gillette Cup

Kent won the Gillette Cup, cricket's first and most famous one-day competition, for the second time when they beat Lancashire in the 1974 final.

In the rain-delayed final, Kent beat Lancashire, triple champions in 1970, 1971 and 1972, by four wickets.

The victory was clinched by wicket-keeper Alan Knott, who scored a vital 18 runs not out just when Kent seemed to be tottering towards defeat.

Knott's performance earned him the £100 Man of the Match award.

Previous winners
1963: Sussex bt Worcs by 14 runs
1964: Sussex bt Warwicks by 8 wickets
1965: Yorkshire bt Surrey by 175 runs
1966: Warwicks bt Worcs by 5 wickets
1967: Kent bt Somerset by 32 runs
1968: Warwicks bt Sussex by 4 wickets
1969: Yorkshire bt Derbys by 69 runs
1970: Lancs bt Sussex by 6 wickets
1971: Lancs bt Kent by 24 runs
1972: Lancs bt Warwicks by 4 wickets
1973: Gloucs bt Sussex by 40 runs

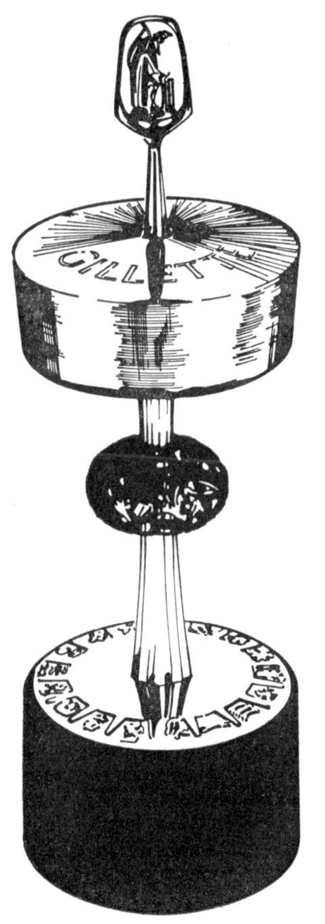
GILLETTE

Gillette Cup – 1975

The first round of the 1975 Gillette Cup will be played on June 25; the second round on July 16. The draw for the first round is: Surrey v. Somerset; Cambs v. Northants; Oxfordshire v. Cornwall; Staffs v. Leics; Notts v. Sussex; Middx. v. Bucks. Second Round Draw: Notts or Sussex v. Kent; Yorkshire or Staffs v. Leics; Gloucs v. Oxfordshire or Cornwall; Surrey or Somerset v. Derbyshire; Warwicks v. Middlesex or Bucks; Lancs. v. Cambridgeshire or Northants; Hampshire v. Glamorgan; Worcestershire v. Essex.

Gillette Cup records

Highest individual score in a Gillette Cup match
Geoff Boycott, who scored 146 for Yorkshire against Surrey in the 1965 final at Lord's.
Highest team total in Gillette Cup match
Gloucestershire, who scored 327 runs for seven wickets against Berkshire at Reading in 1966.

Gillette Cup giant-killers

Only two minor counties sides have beaten County Championship sides in the Gillette Cup – Durham and Lincolnshire.

Durham beat Yorkshire at Harrogate by five wickets in 1973.

In 1974, Lincolnshire beat Glamorgan by six wickets.

Closest Gillette Cup match

Nottinghamshire and Somerset both scored 215 in their match at Taunton in 1964. Somerset went into the next round as they had lost only nine wickets.

Surrey and Sussex both scored 196 runs at the Oval in 1970. Sussex were the winners having lost only eight wickets.

Record partnerships

The record stand by opening batsmen in a Gillette Cup was scored by R. E. Marshall and B. L. Reed who hit 227 runs for Hants against Bedfordshire at Goldington in 1968.

The record stand by a last wicket partnership came from A. T. Castell and D. W. White also of Hants. They scored 45 against Lancashire at Manchester in 1970.

The Benson & Hedges Cup

Surrey became the third winners of the Benson and Hedges Cup, cricket's most recent one-day competition, when they won the 1974 final at Lord's.

They beat Leicestershire by 27 runs, but it was a game that did not live up to the pre-match predictions.

Leicestershire looked to have the game securely under control when they dismissed Surrey for only 170 runs.

But after reaching 46–1, the Midlands side collapsed, losing the next three wickets for only 4 runs.

Surrey's skipper John Edrich won the £100 gold award for the outstanding performance, a decision that surprised many spectators.

He scored 40 runs – Surrey's second highest total of the match – but took 36 overs to do it and hit only two boundaries.

Previous winners
1972: Leicestershire bt Yorkshire by 5 wickets.
1973: Kent bt Worcestershire by 39 runs.

The Benson
and
Hedges Cup

John Player League

A controversy which involved two former England cricket captains – Ray Illingworth and Brian Close – provided a dramatic climax to the 1974 John Player League Championship.

Leicestershire won the title beating Somerset into second place by two points.

But the cold statistics in the record books of the future will hide the full drama of the decisive game which was wrecked by the weather.

Somerset batted first and scored 162 for 9 off 38 overs, but were then accused of 'gamesmanship' by Leicestershire's skipper Illingworth when their final batsman took nearly three minutes to walk from the dressing-room to the crease.

Somerset's Close apologised later, but in the end the alleged time-wasting tactics had no influence on the outcome. The result of the match finally was decided by the weather.

Heavy rain prevented any further play. Both teams were awarded two points for an abandoned game, and that put Leicestershire's six points lead beyond Somerset's reach.

In spite of that controversy, however, most cricket pundits agreed that Leicestershire were worthy winners of the John Player League, and their success following their victory in the 1971 Benson and Hedges Cup establishes them as one of English cricket's outstanding one-day teams.

Previous champions

    1969   –   Lancashire
    1970   –   Lancashire
    1971   –   Worcestershire
    1972   –   Kent
    1973   –   Kent

1974 John Player League Table

		P	W	L	D	A	Pts
Leicester ..	(5)	16	12	1	2	1	54
Somerset ..	(11)	15	11	2	2	0	48
Kent ..	(1)	15	10	3	2	0	44
Northants ..	(17)	16	10	6	0	0	40
Hampshire..	(3)	15	9	5	1	0	38
Sussex ..	(7)	15	8	6	0	1	34
Yorkshire ..	(2)	15	8	6	1	0	34
Middlesex ..	(8)	16	7	7	1	1	32
Surrey ..	(9)	15	7	7	1	0	30
Warwickshire	(16)	15	7	8	0	0	28
Worcestershire	(16)	15	6	7	2	0	28
Lancashire..	(4)	15	5	9	1	1	24
Gloucestershire	(6)	16	4	8	4	0	24
Glamorgan	(14)	15	5	10	0	0	20
Essex ..	(10)	16	4	11	1	0	18
Derbyshire..	(12)	15	4	11	0	0	16
Nottingham-shire ..	(13)	16	3	13	0	0	12

1973 positions in brackets.

1974 first-class averages

Batting

	I	NO	R	H'est	Av
C. H. Lloyd	31	8	1458	178*	63·39
B. Richards	27	4	1406	225*	61·13
G. M. Turner	31	9	1332	202*	60·55
G. Boycott	36	6	1783	160*	59·43
R. T. Virgin	39	5	1936	144*	56·94
D. L. Amiss	31	3	1510	195	53·93
J. H. Edrich	23	2	1126	152*	53·62
J. Hampshire	23	6	901	158	53·00
R. B. Kanhai	22	4	936	213*	52·00
J. A. Jameson	42	2	1932	240*	48·30
G. S. Sobers	27	4	1110	132*	48·26
D. Lloyd	22	2	958	214*	47·90
B. F. Davison	39	3	1670	142	46·38
Zaheer Abbas	30	4	1182	240	45·46
Majid Khan	35	3	1451	164	45·34
B. D'Oliveira	26	3	1026	227*	44·61
M. J. Harris	41	3	1690	133*	44·47
M. J. Smith	38	4	1468	170*	43·18
J. M. Brearley	36	5	1324	173*	42·70
S. Mohammad	32	2	1278	106	42·60
H. Pilling	28	7	869	144	41·38
M. H. Denness	21	2	760	118	40·00
P. J. Watts	33	7	1040	104*	40·00
S. J. Storey	23	4	744	111	39·16
P. J. Graves	39	6	1282	145*	38·85
M. J. K. Smith	38	8	1159	105	38·63
R. D. Knight	40	5	1350	144	38·57
K. W. Fletcher	25	4	809	123*	38·52
M. C. Cowdrey	30	3	1027	122	38·04
R. M. Gilliatt	29	3	977	106	37·58
M. J. Kitchen	24	2	819	88*	37·23
D. B. Close	40	9	1153	114*	37·19

	I	NO	R	H'est	Av
B. Dudleston	41	5	1337	135	37·14
J. Balderstone	23	2	775	140	36·90
R. G. Headley	31	2	1064	137	36·69
L. G. Rowe	30	1	1059	94	36·52
Imran Khan	31	3	1016	170	36·29
D. R. Turner	29	2	977	152	36·19
A. Hill	19	4	539	140*	35·93
L. W. Hill	24	4	718	96	35·90
F. C. Hayes	39	2	1311	187	35·43
A. Kallicharran	39	2	1309	132	35·38
C. Greenidge	33	2	1093	273*	35·26
C. T. Radley	40	5	1231	111*	35·17
K. Snellgrove	17	4	454	75*	34·92
B. R. Hardie	36	2	1168	133	34·35
E. J. Hemsley	15	2	442	120*	34·00
G. R. Roope	33	6	907	119	33·59
M. J. Procter	33	2	1033	157	33·32
P. J. Sainsbury	26	8	599	98	33·28
J. Simmons	25	11	466	75	33·28
S. Turner	33	4	963	118*	33·21
V. A. Richards	38	1	1223	107	33·05
M. J. Smedley	41	6	1134	118*	32·40
F. M. Engineer	26	5	680	108	32·38
B. Luckhurst	35	2	1067	148	32·33
N. Featherstone ..	35	4	996	125	32·13
A. Jones	36	1	1121	113	32·03
M. Mohammad ..	34	3	973	101*	31·39
Younis Ahmed	33	4	907	116	31·28
D. S. Steele	36	3	1022	104	30·97
A. Kennedy	26	2	742	81	30·92
G. Greenidge	42	3	1187	147	30·44
K. S. McEwan	37	2	1056	126	30·17
B. Leadbeater	31	4	804	99*	29·78
C. J. C. Rowe	16	8	237	58*	29·62

	I	NO	R	H'est	Av
G. W. Johnson	37	2	1029	158	29·40
J. M. Parker	27	1	760	140	29·23
G. A. Gooch	25	3	637	114*	28·95
R. Tolchard	35	9	750	103	28·85
R. M. Cooke	29	4	718	100	28·72
P. Thackeray	15	4	315	65*	28·63
T. J. Yardley	31	8	656	66*	28·52
C. J. Aworth	29	2	767	97	28·41
D. J. Taylor	40	5	994	179	28·40
R. A. Woolmer	34	4	840	112	28·00
J. B. Bolus	38	6	892	112	27·88
D. Breakwell	28	7	585	67	27·86
Asif Iqbal	24	2	611	80	27·77
B. Hassan	43	6	1009	83*	27·27
J. T. Murray	28	4	654	82*	27·25
G. P. Howarth	36	2	751	98	26·82
R. G. Willis	22	16	159	24	26·50
J. F. Steele	41	5	953	116*	26·47
C. M. Old	22	2	529	116	26·45
R. G. Lumb	31	2	763	123*	26·31
B. Wood	35	1	893	101	26·26
A. H. Walker	29	1	727	117	25·96
H. Tunnicliffe......	19	5	357	87	25·50
J. Shepherd	30	6	609	79	25·38
D. Shepherd	30	0	747	101	24·90
R. N. Abberley	23	0	567	99	24·65
R. B. Nicholls	23	2	512	68	24·38
D. Nicholls	22	2	487	77	24·35
R. C. Davis	34	3	752	73	24·26
S. J. Rouse	13	3	242	55	24·20
A. W. Stovold	28	1	652	102	24·15
J. Birkenshaw	29	7	530	70*	24·09
G. D. Barlow	21	2	457	70	24·05
M. G. Griffith	20	3	408	121*	24·00

	I	NO	R	H'est	Av
A. W. Greig	28	0	669	106	23·89
E. Hemmings	32	5	645	74	23·89
T. R. Glover	12	1	262	103*	23·81
M. J. J. Faber	28	3	593	112*	23·72
R. Illingworth	27	8	447	67	23·52
F. Swarbrook	32	11	489	65	23·29
P. Willey	37	3	790	100*	23·24
J. M. Parks	36	5	717	66	23·13
T. Cartwright	8	0	185	68	23·12
C. A. Milton	19	1	413	76	22·94
R. Jackman	27	6	431	92*	22·90
A. G. Ealham	33	3	686	73	22·86
Sarfraz Nawaz	21	7	317	53	22·64
J. W. Solanky	25	5	452	71	22·60
G. P. Ellis	18	2	356	116	22·25
M. H. Page	29	0	645	91	22·24
D. L. Murray	34	2	707	78	22·09
T. E. Jesty	28	2	571	90	21·96
N. McVicker	25	5	439	64	21·95
R. I. Smyth	20	0	438	55	21·90
M. N. Taylor	24	2	479	68	21·77
R. E. East	31	6	544	64	21·76
A. R. Lewis	23	1	477	95	21·68
G. Stephenson	24	6	390	69*	21·67
R. D. Butcher	8	1	150	53*	21·42
G. Cook	37	2	746	85	21·31
D. W. Randall	42	4	804	105	21·16
J. D. Morley	43	2	864	85	21·07
B. Edmeades	33	1	673	54*	21·03
J A. Ormrod	34	2	673	82	21·03
Intikhab Alam	28	3	525	61	21·00
A. Tait	20	0	545	99	20·96
K. D. Boyce	16	0	335	75	20·93
B. K. Gardom	20	2	374	79*	20·77

	I	NO	R	H'est	Av
L. E. Skinner	18	0	364	84	20·22
N. G. Cowley	13	1	242	43	20·16
P. Carrick	13	3	196	46	19·60
D. Russell	16	1	291	56*	19·40
A. C. Smith	23	4	368	39	19·37
G. Miller	29	2	518	53	19·19
A. Nicholson	16	8	153	50	19·12
H. Cartwright	11	2	172	43*	19·11
P. H. Edmunds	31	7	453	57	18·88
H. W Wilcock	19	3	302	44	18·88
P. W. Denning	35	1	641	60	18·85
R. A. Hutton	25	5	376	102*	18·80
J. G. Tolchard	25	3	412	64*	18·73
M. Llewellyn	17	0	318	61	18·71
E. W. Jones	30	6	445	67	18·54
E. D. Fursdon	18	5	239	55	18·38
D. L. Bairstow	32	3	533	79	18·38
D. A. Francis	15	5	183	52*	18·30
F. J. Titmus	26	6	366	81*	18·30
P. J. Squires	21	3	329	67*	18·28
R. K. Baker	20	0	364	51	18·20
D. P. Hughes	29	7	399	62	18·14
A. S. Brown	34	2	572	62	17·88
R. V. Lewis	15	1	250	136	17·86
G. I. Burgess	33	0	588	90	17·82
J. A. Snow	34	3	552	63	17·81
G. Sharp	32	7	443	48	17·72
K. Shuttleworth	15	6	159	44	17·66
P J. Sharpe	29	2	474	83	17·56

* Not out.

Bowling

	O	M	R	W	Avge
A. Roberts	727·4	198	1621	119	13·62
G. Arnold	487	139	1069	75	14·25
V. Holder	659	146	1493	94	15·88
M. Procter	311·3	80	776	47	16·51
B. D'Oliveira ..	345·3	105	697	40	17·42
M. Taylor	541	147	1259	72	17·48
H. Moseley ..	661·5	198	1420	81	17·53
R. Illingworth ..	535·1	204	1014	57	17·78
P. Carrick	405·4	167	840	47	17·87
S. Turner	615·5	166	1317	73	18·04
S. Rouse	164·5	34	489	27	18·11
D. Underwood	563	228	1181	65	18·16
R. Baker	207·1	48	494	27	18·30
J. Balderstone	134·4	33	351	19	18·47
G. McKenzie ..	531·3	131	1345	71	18·94
C. M. Old	526·3	132	1366	72	18·97
R. Woolmer	466·4	135	1065	56	19·01
N. Gifford......	617	197	1333	69	19·32
R. Herman	657·3	202	1426	73	19·53
R. Cottam	454	113	1101	56	19·66
M. Hendrick ..	531·1	127	1288	65	19·82
Sarfraz Nawaz ..	559	152	1356	68	19·94
J. Snow	569·1	122	1517	76	19·96
D. Brown	495	134	1143	56	20·41
A. Robinson ..	375·5	103	880	43	20·47
D. Close	104	31	287	14	20·50
B. Wood	405·4	136	892	43	20·74
R. Jackman	669·1	146	1744	84	20·76
B. Brain	633·1	121	1752	84	20·86
Mushtaq Mohammad ..	370·3	102	1106	53	20·87
A. Ward	400·4	82	1174	56	20·96
J. Price	153	33	451	21	21·47

	O	M	R	W	Avge
Asif Iqbal	84	21	215	10	21·50
D. Graveney ..	384·5	105	1014	47	21·57
G. Cope	738·5	260	1681	77	21·83
J. Dye	541·1	110	1512	69	21·91
J. Inchmore	283·2	55	858	39	22·00
E. Hemmings ..	738	213	1855	84	22·08
R. Willis	471·2	92	1369	62	22·08
F. Titmus	941·2	312	1953	88	22·19
N. McVicker ..	511·1	113	1357	61	22·25
B. Langford	412·1	153	937	42	22·31
T. Cartwright ..	273	130	493	22	22·41
A. Jones	565	122	1539	67	22·97
M. Nash	539·5	124	1463	63	23·22
P. Sainsbury....	425·2	196	813	35	23·23
R. White	709·4	197	1909	79	24·16
A. Hodgson	285·2	63	751	31	24·22
G. Miller	380	90	1020	42	24·29
P. Edmonds	815·5	266	1888	77	24·52
P. Lever	562·1	142	1401	57	24·58
B. Bedi.........	1085·3	307	2758	112	24·63
H. Latchman ..	351·3	66	1158	47	24·64
K. Boyce	313·4	55	868	35	24·80
M. Buss	350	122	797	32	24·91
A. Nicholson ..	471	152	1100	44	25·00
S. Storey	108	48	401	16	25·06
Intikhab Alam ..	489·1	120	1459	58	25·16
J. Simmons	602·1	178	1466	58	25·28
K. Higgs	421·1	107	996	39	25·54
R. Hutton	259·2	70	620	24	25·83
I. Botham	309	76	779	30	25·96
W. Taylor	303·5	58	885	34	26·03
P. Pocock	651·5	192	1576	60	26·26
E. Fursdon	330·3	79	870	33	26·36
A. Brown	348·4	86	925	35	26·43

	O	M	R	W	Avge
J. Spencer	464·3	110	1243	47	26·45
G. Johnson ..	468·2	140	1172	44	26·64
K. Shuttleworth	566·1	162	1419	53	26·77
G. Roope	315·2	76	857	32	26·78
J. Birkenshaw	514·2	135	1262	47	26·85
P. Booth	124·5	17	380	14	27·14
G. Phillipson ..	189	50	439	16	27·44
A. Butcher	191·1	42	495	18	27·50
D. Wilson	157·4	39	469	17	27·58
B. Stead	628	147	1713	62	27·63
T. Lamb	395·5	87	997	36	27·69
G. Burgess	437·1	114	1140	41	27·80
D. Hughes	593·3	196	1428	51	28·00
A. C. Smith	291·4	70	729	26	28·04
J. Cumbes	243·5	49	595	21	28·33
R. East	571·1	151	1431	50	28·62
T. Jesty	321·1	96	749	26	28·81
K. Jones	278·5	69	773	27	28·81
D. Williams	511	93	1586	55	28·84
J. Steele	397·5	136	866	30	28·86
J. Graham	465·5	107	1138	39	29·18
M. Vernon	155	19	586	20	29·30
C. Milburn	146	29	353	12	29·41
Sadiq Mohammad ..	92	24	328	11	29·81
Imran Khan	614·2	126	1808	60	30·13
A. Cordle	288·3	41	914	30	30·46
A. Greig	551·5	122	1677	55	30·49
J. Shepherd ..	641	154	1691	55	30·75
P. Lee	342·2	85	902	29	31·10
D. Steele	161	59	405	13	31·15
R. Hobbs	368·1	98	1061	34	31·21
J. Davey	286	46	812	26	31·23
G. Sobers	350·4	79	925	29	31·90

	O	M	R	W	Avge
P. Russell	554·3	154	1412	44	32·09
B. Edmeades	170·4	35	419	13	32·23
R. Knight	388·3	88	1127	34	33·15
C. Waller	582·5	151	1580	47	33·62
W. Blenkiron	160·4	34	473	14	33·78
W. Bourne	166	29	578	17	34·00
P. Wilkinson	377·1	97	953	28	34·04
M. Field	268·4	51	827	24	34·45
D. Breakwell	345·1	108	957	27	35·44
M. Selvey	414·3	82	1246	35	35·60
K. Stevenson	171·2	16	654	18	36·33
J. Solanky	290	59	880	24	36·66
R. Elms	290·4	68	870	23	37·83
S. Venkataraghavan	667·2	136	1913	49	39·04
D. Acfield	303·2	82	709	18	39·38
P. Willey	238·1	69	597	15	39·80
B. Gardom	195·2	31	696	17	40·94

Series Editor: Peter Arnold
Designed by Outline Art Services Limited,
Ashford, Middlesex

Published by
The Hamlyn Publishing Group Limited
London · New York · Sydney · Toronto
Astronaut House, Feltham, Middlesex, England

ISBN 0 600 31896 6

Printed in England by
Cox & Wyman Ltd
London, Fakenham and Reading